THE BIG SLEEP

THE BIG SLEEP

David Baird

MQP

Published by MQ Publications Limited

12 The Ivories
6–8 Northampton Street
London, N1 2HY
Tel: +44 (0)20 7359 2244
Fax: +44 (0)20 7359 1616
E-mail: mail@mqpublications.com

North American Office

49 West 24th Street
8th Floor
New York, NY 10010
E-mail: information@mqpublicationsus.com

Web site: www.mqpublications.com

Copyright © 2006 MQ Publications Limited
Text copyright © 2006 David Baird

ISBN: 1-84601-137-X
ISBN 13: 978-1-84601-137-5

1 2 3 4 5 6 7 8 9

Printed in China

A RUFFLED MIND MAKES A RESTLESS PILLOW.

Charlotte Brontë

How do people go to sleep?
I'm afraid I've lost the knack.
I might try busting myself
smartly over the temple with
the night-light.
I might repeat to myself,
slowly and soothingly,
a list of quotations beautiful
from minds profound; if I can
remember any of the
damn things.

Dorothy Parker

"God help me.
I'm so tired. I need my sleep.
I make no bones about it.
I need eight hours a day,
and at least ten at night."

Bill Hicks

I know a bank whereon
the wild thyme blows,
Where oxlips and the nodding
violet grows,
Quite over-canopied with
luscious woodbine,
With sweet musk-roses,
and with eglantine:
There sleeps Titania
sometime of the night,
Lull'd in these flowers with
dances and delight.

William Shakespeare

ONLY A LITTLE HOLIDAY OF SLEEP,
SOFT SLEEP, SWEET SLEEP; A LITTLE SOOTHING PSALM
OF SLUMBER FROM THY SANCTUARIES OF CALM,
A LITTLE SLEEP—IT MATTERS NOT HOW DEEP;
A LITTLE FALLING FEATHER FROM THY WING,
MERCIFUL LORD—IS IT SO GREAT A THING?

Richard Le Gallienne

Laugh and the world laughs with you, snore and you sleep alone.

Anthony Burgess

A GOOD LAUGH AND A LONG SLEEP ARE THE BEST CURES IN THE DOCTOR'S BOOK.

Irish proverb

Oh sleep! it is a gentle thing, Beloved from pole to pole.

Samuel Taylor Coleridge

Night is a dead monotonous period under a roof; but in the open world it passes lightly, with its stars and dews and perfumes, and the hours are marked by changes in the face of nature.

Robert Louis Stevenson

IF YOU GET A REPUTATION AS AN EARLY RISER, YOU CAN SLEEP TILL NOON.

Irish proverb

We lay stretched upon
the fragrant heath,
and lulled by sound,
Of far-off torrents
charming the still night,
And, to tired limbs
and over-busy thoughts,
Inviting sleep and
soft forgetfulness.

William Wordsworth

As an eagle, weary after soaring in the sky, folds its wings and flies down to rest in its nest, so does the shining Self enter the state of dreamless sleep, where one is freed from all desires.

Brihadaranyaka Upanishad

THERE NEVER WAS A CHILD SO LOVELY, BUT HIS MOTHER WAS GLAD TO GET HIM ASLEEP.

Ralph Waldo Emerson

I divide my time as follows: half the time I sleep, the other half I dream.
I never dream when I sleep, for that would be a pity, for sleeping is the highest accomplishment of genius.

Søren Kierkegaard

i love sleep.
My life has the
tendency to fall apart
when i'm awake,
you know?

Ernest Hemingway

We are such stuff
as dreams are
made on; and our
little life is
rounded with
a sleep.

William Shakespeare

O bed! O bed!
delicious bed!
That heaven upon
earth to the
weary head.

Thomas Hood

THE BED IS A BUNDLE OF PARADOXES: WE GO TO IT WITH RELUCTANCE, YET WE QUIT IT WITH REGRET; WE MAKE UP OUR MINDS EVERY NIGHT TO LEAVE IT EARLY, BUT WE MAKE UP OUR BODIES EVERY MORNING TO KEEP IT LATE.

Charles Caleb Colton

The long day's task is done, And we must sleep.

William Shakespeare

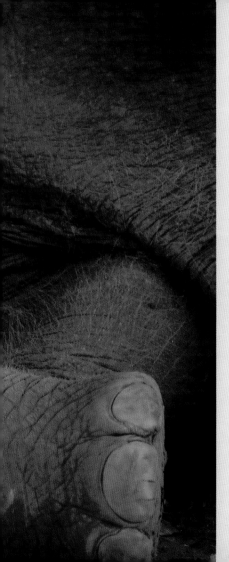

SILENCE IS THE SLEEP THAT NOURISHES WISDOM.

Francis Bacon

Now, blessings
light on him
that first
invented sleep!

Miguel de Cervantes

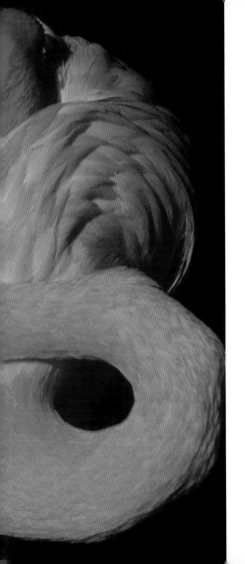

**O magic sleep!
O comfortable bird,
That broodest
o'er the troubled
sea of the mind
Till it is hush'd
and smooth!**

John Keats

PEACE, PEACE, THOU OVER-ANXIOUS, FOOLISH HEART,
REST, EVER-SEEKING SOUL, CALM, MAD DESIRES,
QUIET, WILD DREAMS THIS IS THE TIME OF SLEEP.

Leolyn Louise Everett

Enjoy the honey-heavy
dew of slumber.
Thou hast no figures,
nor no fantasies,
Which busy care draws
in the brains of men;
Therefore thou
sleep'st so sound.

William Shakespeare

**Sleep, sleep, beauty bright,
Dreaming in the joys of night.**

William Blake

No day is so bad
it can't be fixed
with a nap.

Carrie Snow

IF YOU WANT YOUR DREAMS TO COME TRUE, DON'T OVER SLEEP.

Yiddish proverb

Fatigue is the best pillow.

Benjamin Franklin

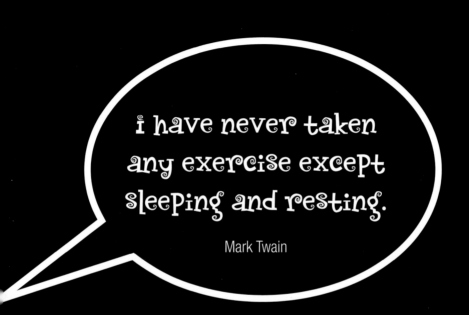

SLEEPING ALONE, EXCEPT UNDER DOCTOR'S ORDERS, DOES MUCH HARM. CHILDREN WILL TELL YOU HOW LONELY IT IS SLEEPING ALONE. IF POSSIBLE, YOU SHOULD ALWAYS SLEEP WITH SOMEONE YOU LOVE. YOU BOTH RECHARGE YOUR MUTUAL BATTERIES FREE OF CHARGE.

Marlene Dietrich

The rich mind lies in the sun and sleeps, and is Nature.

Ralph Waldo Emerson

IT'S AMAZING WHEN YOU GET TO A CERTAIN AGE, AND YOU TALK ABOUT SLEEP IN THE SAME WAY YOU SPOKE ABOUT GETTING INEBRIATED... I GOT EIGHT HOURS LAST NIGHT. IT WAS FANTASTIC!

Johnny Depp

A well-spent day brings happy sleep.

Leonardo da Vinci

WHAT HATH NIGHT TO DO WITH SLEEP?

John Milton

The best cure for insomnia is to get a lot of sleep.

W. C. Fields

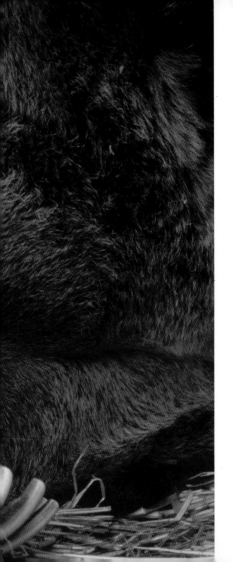

Twenty gallons
of balmy sleep,
Dreamless, and deep,
and mild,
Of the excellent brand
you used to keep
When I was a
little child.

Agnes L. Storrie

FINISH EACH DAY BEFORE YOU BEGIN THE NEXT, AND INTERPOSE A SOLID WALL OF SLEEP BETWEEN THE TWO. THIS YOU CANNOT DO WITHOUT TEMPERANCE.

Ralph Waldo Emerson

Sunsets and evening shadows find me regretful at tasks undone, but sleep and the dawn and the air of the morning touch me with freshening hopes. Strange things blow in through my window on the wings of the night wind and I don't worry about my destiny.

Carl Sandburg

THE WATCHFUL MOTHER TARRIES NIGH, THOUGH SLEEP HAS CLOSED HER INFANTS' EYES.

John Keble

I must down to the seas again,
to the vagrant gypsy life,
To the gull's way and the whale's way
where the wind's like a whetted knife
And all I ask is a merry yarn from
a laughing fellow rover,
And quiet sleep and a sweet dream
when the long trick's over.

John Masefield

Picture Credits

p. 6 and 58 © Maximilian Weinzierl / Alamy; p. 8 and p. 36 © David A. Northcott/CORBIS; p. 10 © age fotostock/SuperStock; p. 12 © age fotostock/SuperStock; p. 15 © Yann Arthus-Bertrand/CORBIS; p. 16 © Martin Harvey; Gallo Images/CORBIS; p. 19 © Maximilian Weinzierl / Alamy; p. 20 © William Manning/CORBIS; p. 23 © Martin Harvey/CORBIS; p. 24 © Dan Guravich/CORBIS; p. 27 © Staffan Widstrand/CORBIS; p. 28 © Buddy Mays/CORBIS; p. 31 © Fotosonline / Alamy; p. 32 © Joe McDonald/CORBIS; p. 35 © Reuters/CORBIS; p. 39 © age fotostock/SuperStock; p. 40 © DK Limited/CORBIS; p. 42 © age fotostock/SuperStock; p. 44 © Gallo Images/CORBIS; p. 47 © Kevin Schafer/CORBIS; p. 48 © Thai-Images / Alamy; p. 51 © age footstock/SuperStock; p. 52 © Kevin Schafer/zefa/Corbis; p. 54 © Jim Craigmyle/CORBIS; p. 56 © Akira Matoba/SuperStock; p. 61 © Raymond Gehman/CORBIS; p. 63 © Darrell Gulin/CORBIS; p.65 © Kevin Schafer/CORBIS; p. 66 © Michael & Patricia Fogden/CORBIS; p. 69 © Carl & Ann Purcell/CORBIS; p. 70 © age fotostock/SuperStock; p. 73 © Ric Ergenbright/CORBIS; p. 74 © Tom Brakefield/CORBIS; p. 77 © AM Corporation / Alamy; p. 78 © Julie Habel/CORBIS; p. 81 © Martin Harvey; Gallo Images/CORBIS; p. 82 © Ralph A. Clevenger/CORBIS; p. 84 © Charles Krebs/CORBIS; p. 86 © Kennan Ward/CORBIS; p. 89 © Joe McDonald/CORBIS; p. 90 © Kevin Schafer/CORBIS

Text Credits

p. 68 extract from Marlene Dietrich's ABC by Marlene Dietrich (Doubleday 1962); p. 87 © Carl Sandburg